IMAGES
*of America*

# MARTINEZ

# IMAGES
## *of America*
# MARTINEZ

Martinez Historical Museum

ARCADIA
PUBLISHING

Published by Arcadia Publishing
Charleston, South Carolina


Library of Congress Catalog Card Number: 2004106920

For all general information contact Arcadia Publishing at:
Telephone 843-853-2070
Fax 843-853-0044
E-mail sales@arcadiapublishing.com
For customer service and orders:
Toll-Free 1-888-313-2665

Visit us on the Internet at www.arcadiapublishing.com

The intersection of Ferry and Main Streets has been the hub of downtown Martinez since 1850. This photograph of a sign over Main Street, looking toward Ferry Street, was taken around 1930.

# CONTENTS

# ACKNOWLEDGMENTS

The publications committee of the Martinez Historical Society—John Curtis, Paul Kraintz, Richard Patchin, Ruth Sutter, and Kathy Yates—selected the photographs and gathered information for the text. Ruth Sutter prepared the text.

The materials for this book have been drawn from the collections of the Martinez Historical Society, archived at the society's museum. We wish to thank museum volunteers Leah Caldarazzo, Dunstan Granshaw, Colleen Inzerillo, Emma Kolokousis, and Marlene Thompson for their contributions to this project. We thank also Justine Sellick, immediate past director of the museum, and Andrea Blachman, present director, for their help.

# INTRODUCTION

Places that come within the orbit of metropolitan centers often lose their distinctiveness. They become suburbs, and the suburbs merge, so that a traveler might recognize one or another of them only by a "now entering" sign.

Martinez is in the economic orbit of Oakland and San Francisco and has been for many years. Yet it has not lost its identity. This book illustrates the maintaining of its identity despite physical changes and despite changes in its economic role and population over the years.

Before Martinez was a place on maps, people passed through the area to reach the Carquinez Strait: Native Americans first and then, in the 1770s, Spanish explorers. Mapping began with grants of land by the independent Mexican government: one to Don Ignacio Martinez (1842), another to William Welch (1844).

Within the Martinez grant, the mouth of Alhambra Creek became a place from which to cross the strait in 1847, when Robert Semple established the first regular ferry service in the Bay Area. Two years later the Martinez-Benicia ferry became an essential route to the gold fields of the Sierra Nevada. William M. Smith, who married into the Martinez family, saw that the ferry traffic could support a town. He arranged for surveys, invited investors from San Francisco, and called the new place Martinez.

Prospectors and businessmen stopped here, and some of them stayed to build hotels and stores and homes or to farm in an area that one of the settlers referred to as "a perfect paradise." It was the only significant town on East Bay maps when the California legislature divided the state into counties in 1851. It named Martinez the county seat for Contra Costa, and residents made plans for county offices and courts.

Its deep-water port made the town a center for maritime shipping. Wheat from the Alhambra, Reliez, and Diablo Valleys was the most important export at first. Growers established a chapter of the Patrons of Husbandry (Grange) and built a wharf near the ferry terminal in 1877. A leader in this work, Dr. John T. Strentzel, also pioneered in the development of orchard crops. He attracted others with his methods, and a naturalist who visited him—John Muir—married his daughter in 1880 and made Martinez his home base.

Fishing was a second economic mainstay. It was pioneered by Sicilian and Italian immigrants in the 1870s and 1880s, among them the DiMaggio family whose sons became baseball legends. In addition to fishing and canneries, Italian and Portuguese families established wineries in Martinez, one of which is still in production.

Railroad companies built Bay Area and Northern California connections that included Martinez. Links to the San Joaquin Valley and Oakland gave Martinez a place in international grain transportation. It became an official station on the transcontinental line.

It was not just a county seat but also a county center. Retail outlets and the offices of physicians, dentists, and pharmacists drew people to Martinez from the surrounding agricultural areas. So did churches and schools. John Swett, the founder of California's public school system, who retired in Alhambra Valley, was instrumental in organizing the Alhambra Union High School District. Newspapers, a library, and social organizations also helped to develop and maintain a sense of community in Martinez.

The main utilities—water, sewers, electricity—and telephone service were available at the turn of the 20th century. James Borland (son-in-law of the builder of the house that later inspired formation of the Martinez Historical Society) was an innovator in establishing these services.

The builders of Martinez adopted and adapted architectural styles of the times. The first Spanish-Mexican adobes were followed by houses constructed with redwood from the forest in the Oakland hills. In the late 19th and early 20th centuries builders often used Victorian styles, as can still be seen on Martinez streets. Distinctive residential neighborhoods developed, too: Vine Hill, Island Hill, an Italian enclave around lower Alhambra Creek, Mountain View, and Portuguese Flats.

Until the 1910s most industry in Martinez was small in scale. Mountain Copper Smelter, established above Bull's Head Point in 1905, smelted metals and produced fertilizers. But refineries, especially the Shell Oil plant established in 1915, gave industry in Martinez a new dimension, and housing for the increased population began to spread southward.

Continued expansion to the south since the 1950s has blurred the lines between the outskirts of town and the housing developments of neighboring bedroom communities. At the same time, people employed at the refineries and by the county government have found homes further and further away from their work, and the highways in and out of the Martinez area have become crowded with commuters.

After World War I, Prohibition depressed the wine industry and salmon fishing was abolished. Later legislation against gill and trammel nets ended commercial fishing in the strait and delta. The railroad ferry went out of business when the railroad bridge was completed (1930). An automobile bridge (1962) ended auto and passenger ferry service. Highways 4 and 680 took travelers past Martinez rather than through the town. However, Amtrak took over passenger rail service (1971), and the city built a new depot (2001) near the old one close to downtown.

In spite of these changes, a core has remained, a downtown. Martinez is one of the few local communities in the Bay Area that still has an intact downtown district. It has been centered at Ferry and Main Streets for more than 150 years.

In the 21st century Martinez is the location of Contra Costa County's governmental offices and courts, a variety of social institutions and organizations, the Contra Costa County Community College District, and both the Contra Costa County and the Martinez Historical Societies.

The Borland Home, the Victorian-era home of the Martinez Historical Society's museum and archives, illustrates the continuity of community identity in itself. Its collection of information about the past provides a foundation for understanding the present and for shaping the future of the community of Martinez.

# One

# A PLACE ON THE MAP

The place called Martinez had just a few buildings and residents in 1851 when the state legislature designated it as the county seat for Contra Costa County, including land that was later separated into Alameda County. Within a year, however, citizens signed a petition for incorporation. Their petition described an area of one square mile with its base a quarter mile from the high water mark of the Strait of Carquinez. This aerial view shows the town, situated on the shore of the strait across from Benicia, as it had developed by the mid-20th century. As maps show, the outlines and extent of Martinez have changed over time. The first maps were of Mexican land grants. Then came surveys and maps to plot land ownership. Road and street maps are the ones most commonly used to define places today.

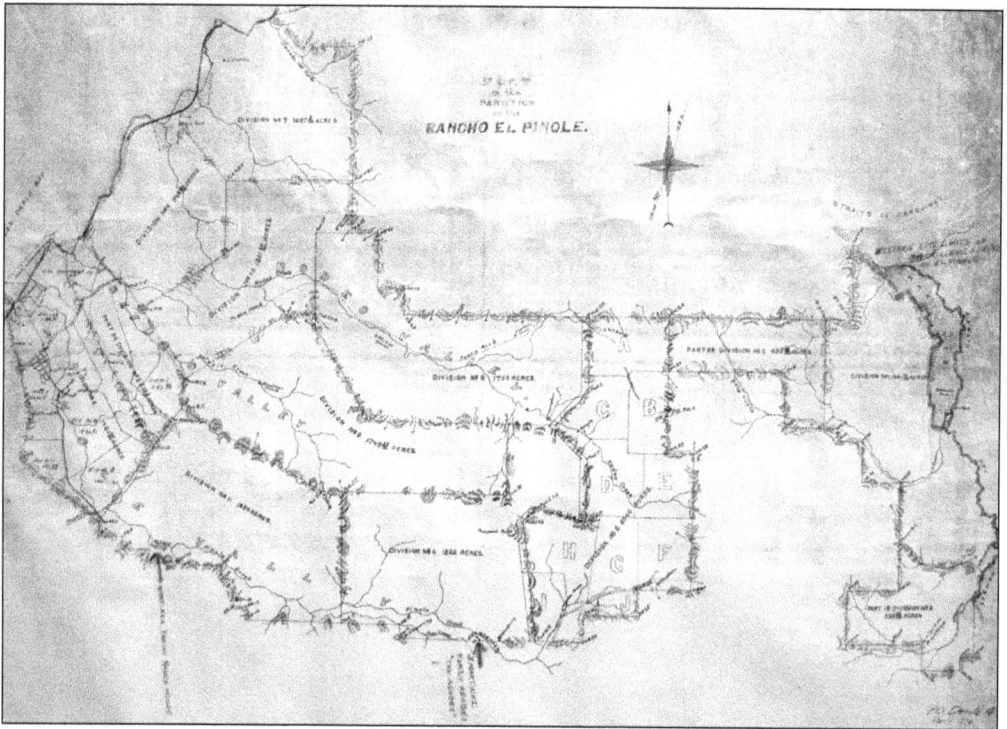

Following the practice established by Spain in the New World, Mexico granted land to soldiers on its frontiers when it became independent. Don Ignacio Martinez, commander of the Presidio in San Francisco, petitioned the government for four leagues, or more than 17,000 acres, in 1824. His sons and daughters built homes and pastured cattle on land along the strait west of Alhambra Creek. The grant, Rancho el Pinole, was affirmed in 1842.

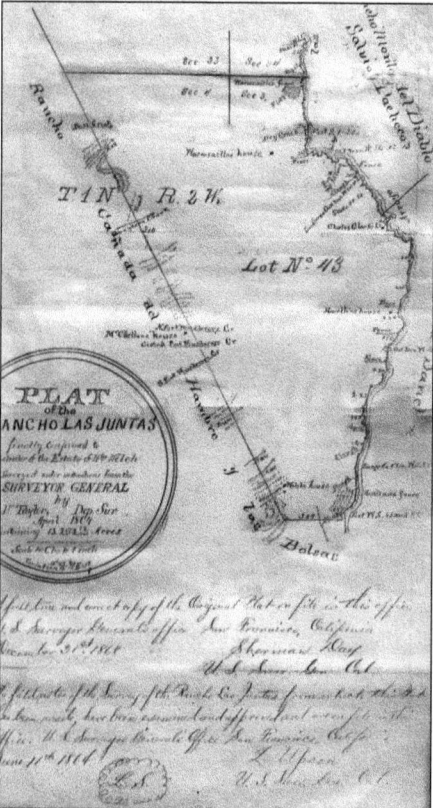

William Welch, a Scottish sailor who jumped ship in California in 1821, asked for a grant of his own to raise cattle and received three leagues, or more than 13,000 acres, east of Alhambra Creek, affirmed in 1844. This land became Rancho las Juntas. The surveyors drew the boundaries of the ranchos as shown here in 1849 and 1854.

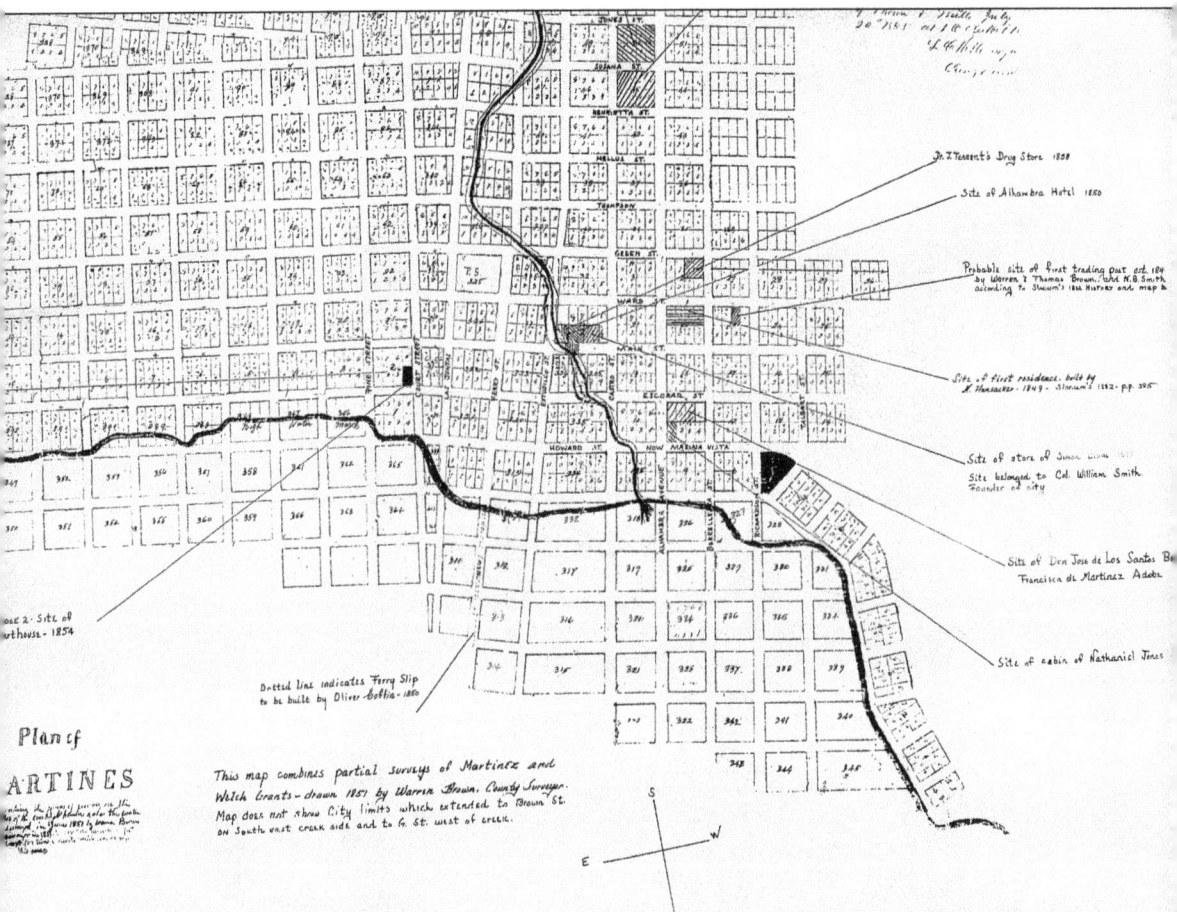

One of Ignacio Martinez's daughters, Susana, married Col. William M. Smith, who served in the war with Mexico. Seeing the potential for a town where a ferry crossed the Carquinez Strait (see chapter two), he persuaded the Martinez heirs to agree to a survey of the land along the waterfront. His dream was to develop a commercial center to rival San Francisco. Thomas A. Brown and his brother Warren completed the survey in 1849 and made an additional survey for lots east of the creek at the request of the Welch family. This map of the surveyed lots was drawn in 1887, and features of the town at that time were indicated in the margins.

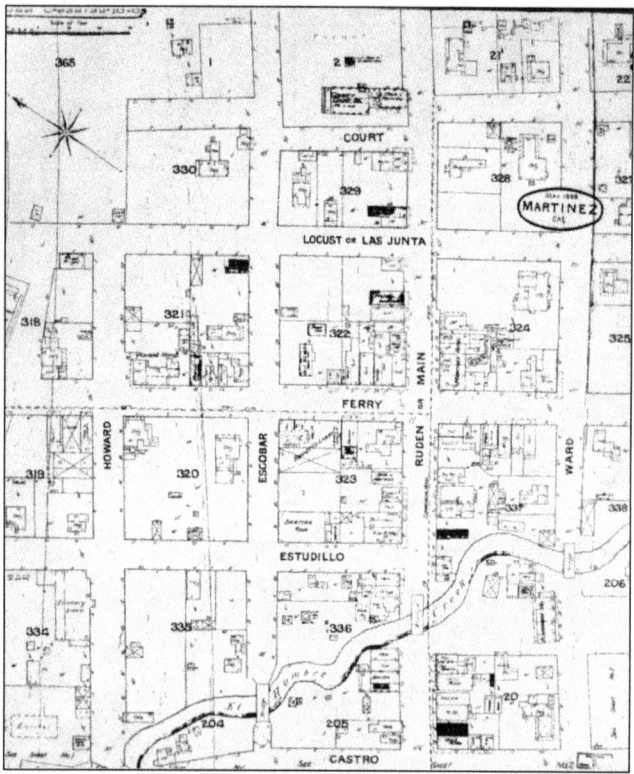

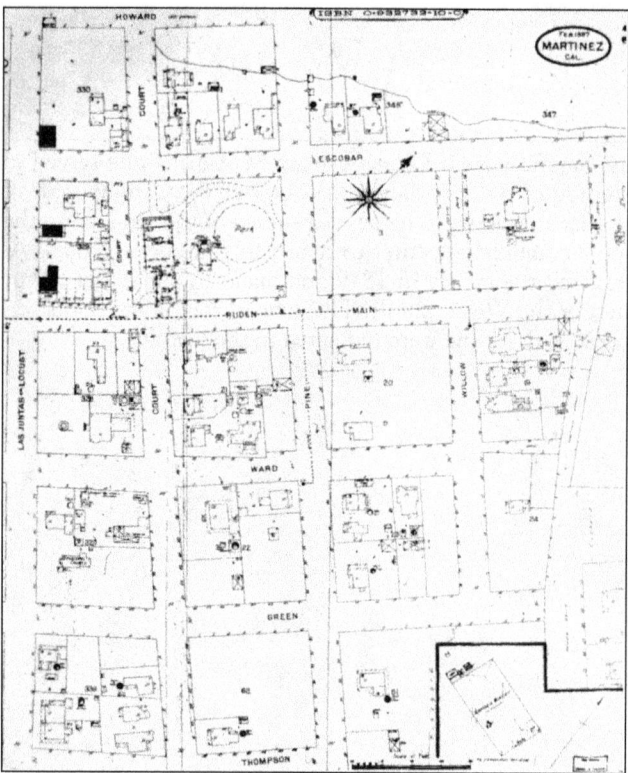

Sanborn Fire Insurance Company maps are detailed plottings of lots, showing outlines of buildings, that were drawn for insurance purposes. Note in these examples from 1888 (above, upper left) and 1897 (below, upper right) that a vacant lot next to the courthouse became a park, as depicted on page 13.

The park that was laid out between 1888 and 1897 turned the courthouse block into a town square or plaza, potentially a social as well as a governmental center for Martinez. This was the first park in Martinez, which later became a city of parks.

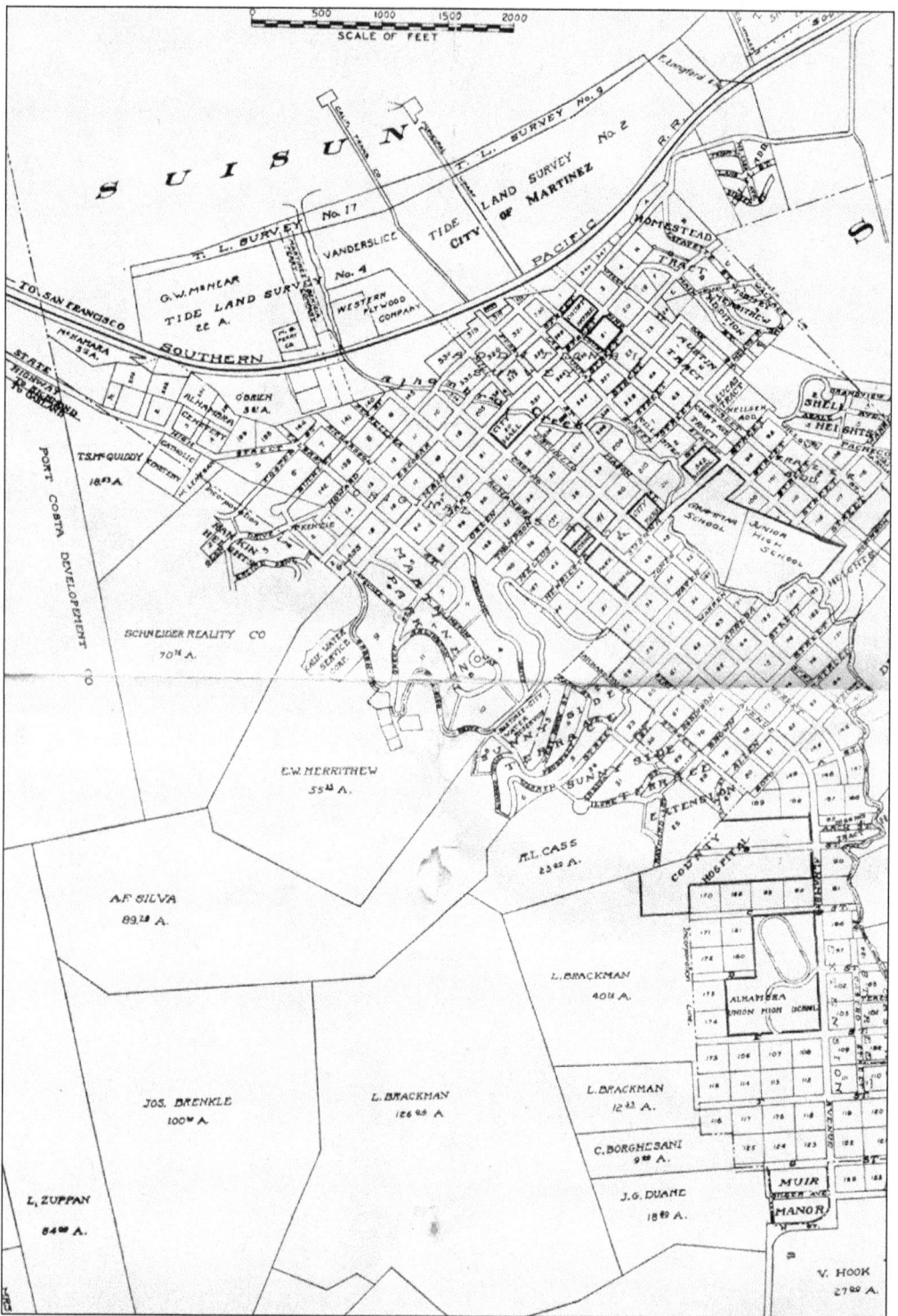

This map, published by the Martinez Chamber of Commerce in 1930, shows the town lots as well as surveyed tidelands and outlying agricultural properties.

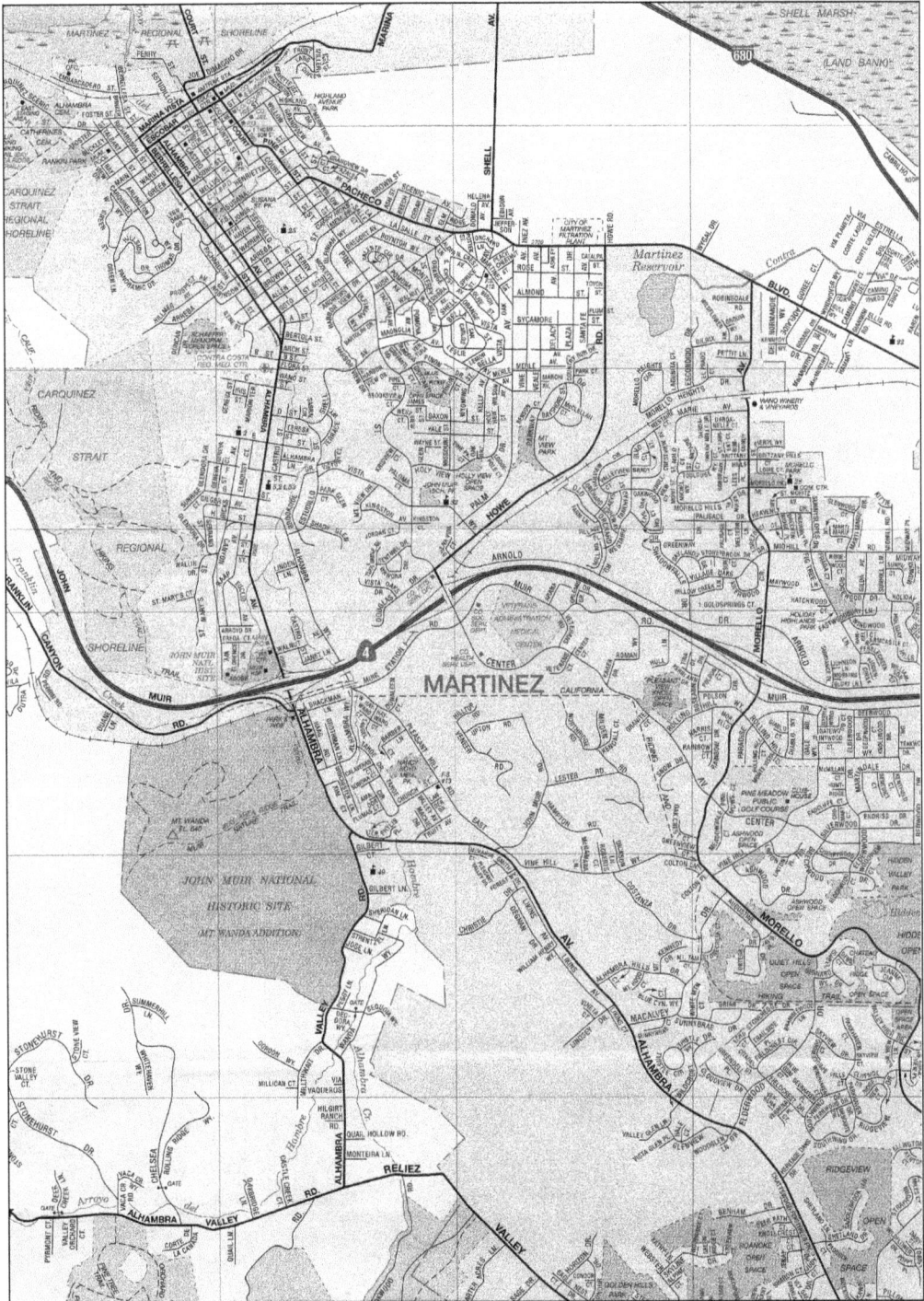

This road map of Martinez was published in 2004. Annexations, especially from the 1960s to the 1990s, greatly expanded the area of the city.

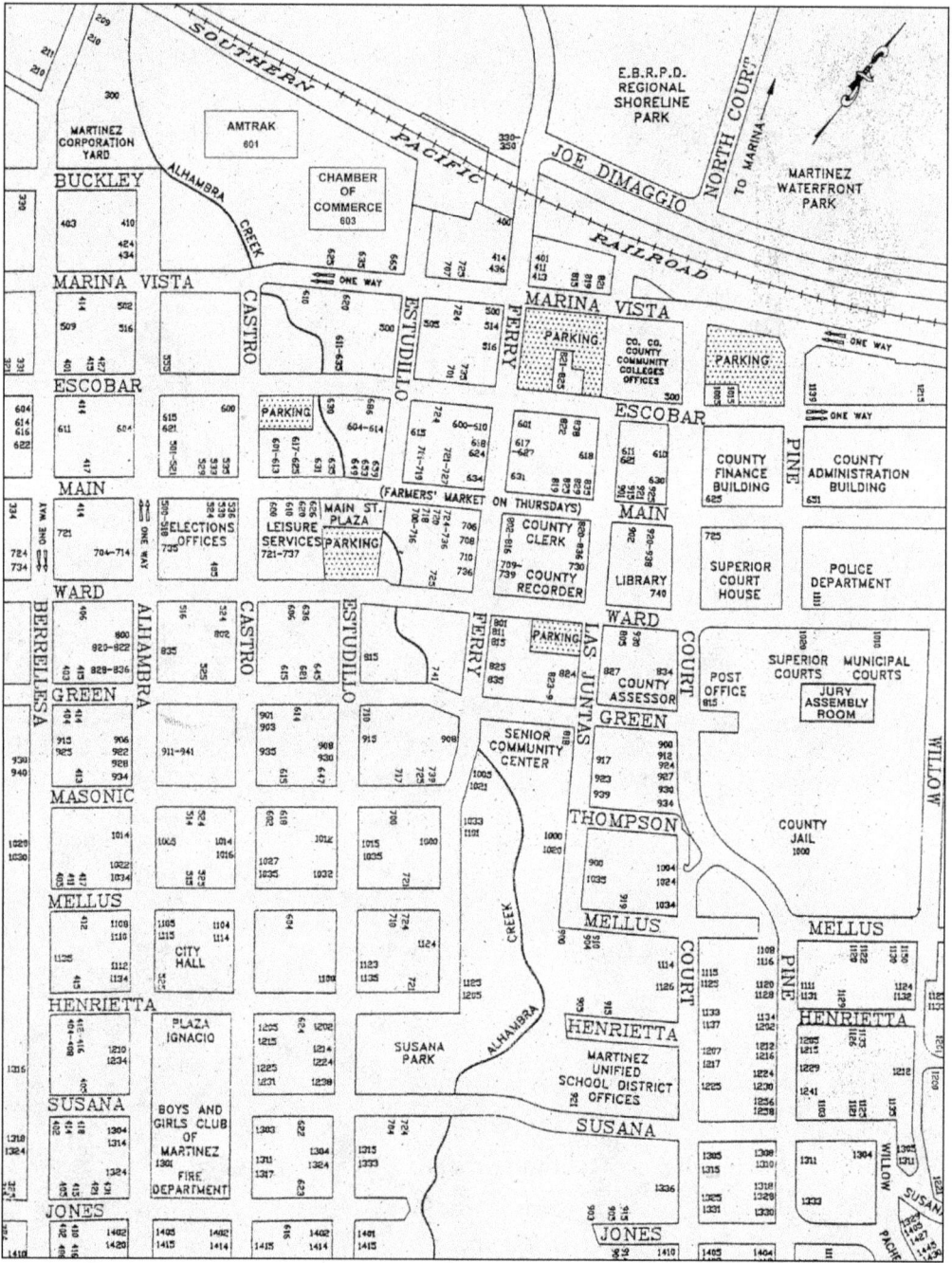

This is the most recent chamber of commerce map of the downtown streets.

16

# Two

# A PLACE IN CALIFORNIA'S HISTORY

California's legislature gave Martinez a place in the state's history when it made the town a county seat. To show its prominence, county officers found a site for the courthouse on a rise and oriented the building to face the waterfront (off to the right in this photograph). The waterfront, with the harbor and regular ferry traffic, spurred the town's early economy and tied it to the state's economic history. This photograph, taken in 1857, is the earliest on record.

17

The first courthouse was a two-story brick and frame building with a small bell tower. This classical style of architecture was a common choice for public structures in the western United States in the mid-19th century. A bell, shipped from New York in 1855, was used to call the court into session, to announce that verdicts had been reached, and to sound the alarm for a fire.

In 1901 the county supervisors voted to replace the first courthouse with a larger building. They gave the contract to the Pacific Construction Company, which had built several courthouses in Northern California, and hired architects from the Havens and Toepke firm in San Francisco. Granite for the exterior came from quarries in Madera County. Two years later the townspeople gathered to celebrate its completion. In a rare photograph, the two buildings are shown together, before the demolition of the older building.

COURT HOUSE, MARTINEZ, CALIF. 5386

The 1903 courthouse had a more elaborate dome than the first courthouse; however, the same bell was used in both. Both the dome and the bell were removed in 1957 when officials worried about safety during an earthquake. The bell is now in the Martinez Museum.

Carquinez Strait, shown here in an early photograph, connects San Francisco Bay and its northern extension, San Pablo Bay, with Suisun Bay to the east. The Sacramento and San Joaquin Rivers flow through the strait. It is about eight miles long and one mile wide at its narrowest part. Robert Semple, who became an important participant in California's constitutional convention in 1849, operated the first ferry service, commissioned by Gen. Mariano Vallejo, across the Carquinez Strait, in 1847. Within a year of the discovery of gold on the American River in 1848, the southern shore became crowded with eager passengers and competing ferries were launched. Oliver Coffin and Seth Swain obtained a franchise for ferry service between Martinez and Benicia in 1850. They placed a steam-powered ferry in service the following year.

The ferry *Carquinez* was a double-end, dual paddle-wheeler modeled after the Brooklyn Ferry (above). It ran between Martinez and Benicia from 1854 to 1881. The "walking beam" engine was installed in its successor, the *Benicia* (below), built in 1882. But the waterfront was changing. Silt from hydraulic mining operations in the Sierra foothills was shoaling the shore, so that a wharf became necessary for ferry landings. As early as 1854 Oliver Coffin and his brother built a wharf, the first in Martinez, at the foot of Ferry Street.

In 1879 the Central Pacific Railroad began running a train ferry touted as the largest in the world, the *Solano*, between Benicia and Bull Valley (Port Costa) west of Martinez. A few years later it bought and closed the Martinez ferry (1888), giving the railroad exclusive rights to ferry service across the strait and leaving Martinez without a direct route. Along with trains, the *Solano* and its sister ship *Contra Costa* also carried the early automobiles. The *Solano* is shown here on closing day November 1, 1930.

Anticipating the increasing importance of automobile traffic, Martinez and Benicia businessmen, with the encouragement of Central Pacific directors, organized a new ferry line and opened it on a new municipal wharf in 1913, with much local fanfare. The *Issaquah*, shown below, was used from 1930 to 1940. The auto ferry continued to operate until 1962.

# *Three*

# AN ECONOMIC CENTER

From the 1850s on, wheat growers and orchardists in the fertile valleys around Martinez shipped their produce from its harbor to San Francisco and markets around the world. Alhambra Valley was especially productive well into the 20th century. A second major enterprise was fishing. Fishing and fish canneries became an important part of the town's economy by the 1880s. By then railroads vied with waterways in connecting Martinez to places near and far. Martinez became a commercial as well as a governmental center. Industrial development began with copper smelting, and oil refineries eventually predominated, employing the largest number of workers.

Growers organized a local chapter, or grange, of the national organization of Patrons of Husbandry in 1874. Together with Walnut Creek and Danville granges, they formed an association to construct a warehouse and wharf at the mouth of Alhambra Creek. Wheat was the main crop for shipment at that time, but within a few years much of it was being loaded at Port Costa and carried by the railroad, while fruit crops and nuts were packed and shipped from Martinez. John Strentzel had the most extensive orchards in Alhambra Valley. He experimented with methods of storage and shipping as well as of production of fruit. His work attracted the attention of naturalist John Muir, who married Strentzel's daughter Louie in 1880. In this photograph, Grangers' Wharf is center left; California Transportation Wharf is to its right.

Before highways and railroads were built, agricultural commerce depended on river transportation, such as small packet boats. The steam packet *Onward* is shown here loaded with freight at the California Transportation Company wharf.

Strentzel discovered that produce packed in carbonized bran would stay fresh longer during shipping. This discovery enabled him and others to ship their fruit to distant markets. He also grew grapes and began producing wine as early as the 1860s. By the turn of the 20th century there were a number of vineyards and wineries around Martinez. This photograph shows vineyards that became part of the Digardi winery.

DE LA SALLE INSTITUTE CHRISTIAN BROTHERS MARTINEZ, CAL.

Like Strentzel, Henry Bush grew a variety of fruits and grapes beginning in the 1850s. The Christian Brothers Society of St. Mary's College bought land from his estate in 1879 that included a vineyard. The society built an educational institution, De La Salle Institute, as a novitiate (above) partly from vineyard profits. Leading to the institute was an avenue of cypresses (below). The vineyard became the nucleus of a highly successful winery. Christian Brothers moved its operation to Napa Valley in 1931.

In 1886 the Joost family established a winery in the Vine Hill district south of Martinez, expanding the area of productive vineyards. Frank Digardi bought the property in 1912. His winery became the only one in the Martinez area to survive the Prohibition era. The buildings pictured here were north of Pacheco Boulevard with the Shell refinery on the other side of the hills. The Digardi home, on the left, remains standing today.

Among the Italian families who raised fruit, including grapes, were the Vianos. They turned to wine making, with dry-farmed vines, after World War II. This winery is the only one in Martinez still in operation.

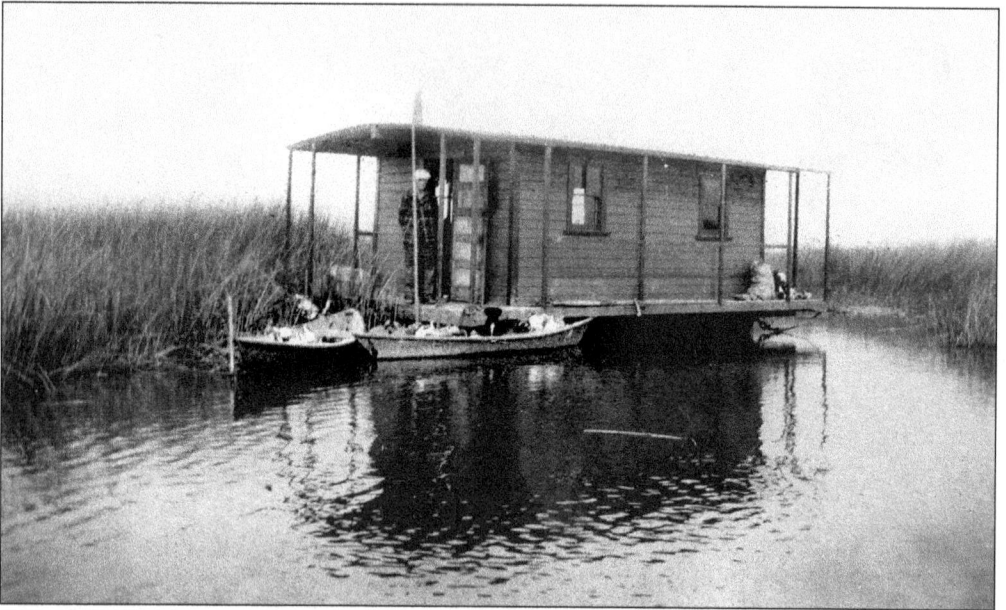

In the 1870s and 1880s Italian fishers began migrating to Northern California. In Martinez, some lived at first in houseboats, or "arks," moored along Alhambra Creek, others in boarding houses, and others in homes west of the creek and Grangers' Wharf. They fished for salmon and shad in the strait and delta as well as the Sacramento River. Two canneries were established near the wharf in 1882: Black's Cannery and the Martinez Packing Company, which employed Chinese workers. They shipped salmon by rail to the eastern United States and on ships to Australia, England, New Zealand, and Honolulu. Pictured above is an example of an ark on Alhambra Creek.

This is a photograph of fishing boats moored in Alhambra Creek at low tide.

This motorized vessel is typical of those used until the end of commercial fishing in the strait.

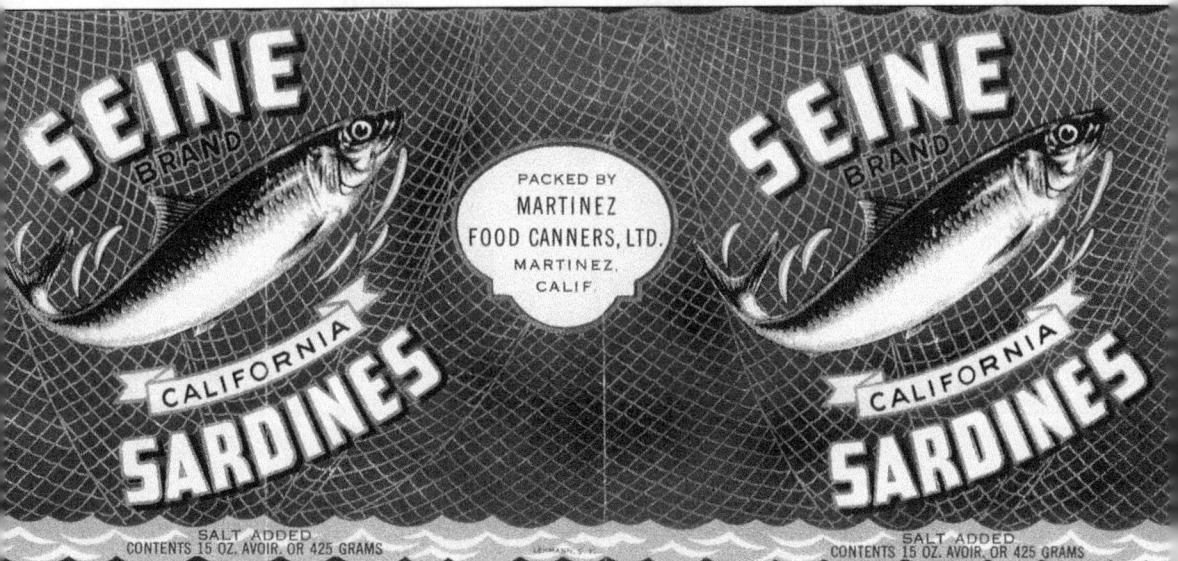

Sardines were brought in to the canneries for processing, packing, and shipping. Pictured here is a label from a can of sardines packed in Martinez. The fishers used seine nets (nets hung vertically in the water), as depicted in the artwork on the label.

Surveyors for a railroad line between Martinez and Fresno County worked on a low-level route along the Carquinez Strait in the early 1870s. They lived in tents along the proposed route of the tracks, moving the tents periodically so that their camps were always close to the area on which they were working. The scene shown here is now part of East Bay Regional Park.

The Northern Railway Company began construction of a line to connect Oakland and Martinez in 1877. It laid tracks to Ferry Street, built an engine house and turntable, and, on the east side of Ferry Street, built a "Swiss-rustic" train station and a water tower. This postcard view was taken in 1909. Martinez became an official stop on the transcontinental line in 1878, but then the Central Pacific Railroad Company turned its attention to ferrying trains across the strait, bypassing Martinez except for the trains to the Central Valley and Southern California.

This is the waiting room as seen in 1915. It was on the first floor with the baggage and freight areas. The stationmaster lived on the second floor.

In the 1890s the Atchison, Topeka & Santa Fe Railway Company built a line between the San Joaquin Valley and Point Richmond, crossing Alhambra Valley south of Martinez on this iron viaduct (later replaced with steel). It passed along the southern edge of the Strentzel-Muir property, and according to a family story, John Muir's daughters sometimes stood in the bell tower of their home to wave at the train engineers.

In this photo a westbound double-headed freight train is crossing the Alhambra trestle. There are vineyards on the slopes in the background.

John Muir and his wife, Louie, who with members of John's family managed the Strentzel orchards after John Strentzel's death, gave land for a station next to the Santa Fe viaduct. A spur, a tributary track off the main line, brought fruit from packing sheds for loading. This photograph was taken around 1940. The station burned the following year.

Railroad companies had been studying the feasibility of bridging the strait since the 1870s. It was not until 1927 that the Southern Pacific Railroad Company, successor to the Central Pacific, made specific plans to construct a bridge between Bull's Head Point in Martinez and Army Point in Benicia. The photograph above left shows the bridge under construction

in 1929. The photograph above right shows the through-truss span section raised for river traffic. Completed in 18 months, this bridge was the longest double-track span west of the Mississippi River.

When the job was done and the first train crossed the new railroad bridge in 1930, a crowd of dignitaries and locals gathered to meet it. With the completion of the Southern Pacific Bridge, Martinez once again became a stop on the transcontinental route.

The growing town required utilities such as a dependable supply of water, gas, and electricity for heating and lighting. James Borland was involved in projects to meet these needs and also in bringing the first telephone service to Martinez. He first installed telephone equipment in the railroad depot in 1881, and when Pacific Bell acquired his company in 1892 he brought in his brother Robert to be general manager. Pacific Bell, based in San Francisco, wanted the superior technology of the Martinez operation. These photographs show the telephone exchange and switchboard in 1907. This building still stands, although it has been extensively remodeled.

William and Henry Hale and Lafayette and Charles Fish founded and built the Bank of Martinez in 1873 to serve the area's farmers. It was the first bank in Contra Costa County and for a time the only one. A fire destroyed the building in August 1904; rebuilt in 1905, it was damaged in the earthquake the following year.

Increasing business needs and opportunities in Martinez brought in capital and investment in new banks such as the First National Bank, which opened in 1904 at Main and Las Juntas Streets.

A new surge of business after Shell Oil Company began operations (1915) brought in new financial institutions such as the American Bank of Oakland, seen here in this photograph taken in the 1920s on the southeast corner of Las Juntas and Main Street during what appears to have been a funeral cortege. A flag flies at half-mast.

The Bank of Martinez, on the corner of Ferry and Main Streets, was one of the few buildings in central Martinez that was badly damaged in the earthquake of 1906. Although the quake of 1868 caused extensive damage to the young town, in 1906 one newspaper reported only "slight" damage, in the amount of $50,000.

The Martinez Gas Company obtained a charter in 1887 and began to supply gas for street lights and homes. It merged with the Contra Costa Gas Company in 1914 and became part of the Coast Counties Gas and Electric Company in 1923, with an office on Ferry Street (at right). Pacific Gas and Electric Company, incorporated in San Francisco in 1905, bought this and other local gas and electric companies over the next few years. Most of the buildings in the center of town had electricity by 1920.

Martinez is one of the few cities of its size in California to have its own water system. Citizens organized a Martinez Water Company in 1883, with sources in the canyons west of town, but ownership of wells and pipes remained in private hands until 1918, when voters passed a bond issue to buy the facilities. In 1941 the Martinez Citizens Water Committee put a bond measure on the ballot for a water treatment plant. The resulting facility on Pacheco Boulevard, shown here, was constructed during the 1950s.

Among the early businesses in Martinez was Lasell's general merchandise store. Loren Marcellus Lasell founded it around 1885 on Smith Street (now Alhambra Avenue), a location thought at the time to be outside the business zone. With success, he expanded it into the largest store in Martinez, advertising 14 departments at one time. It closed in 1989.

44

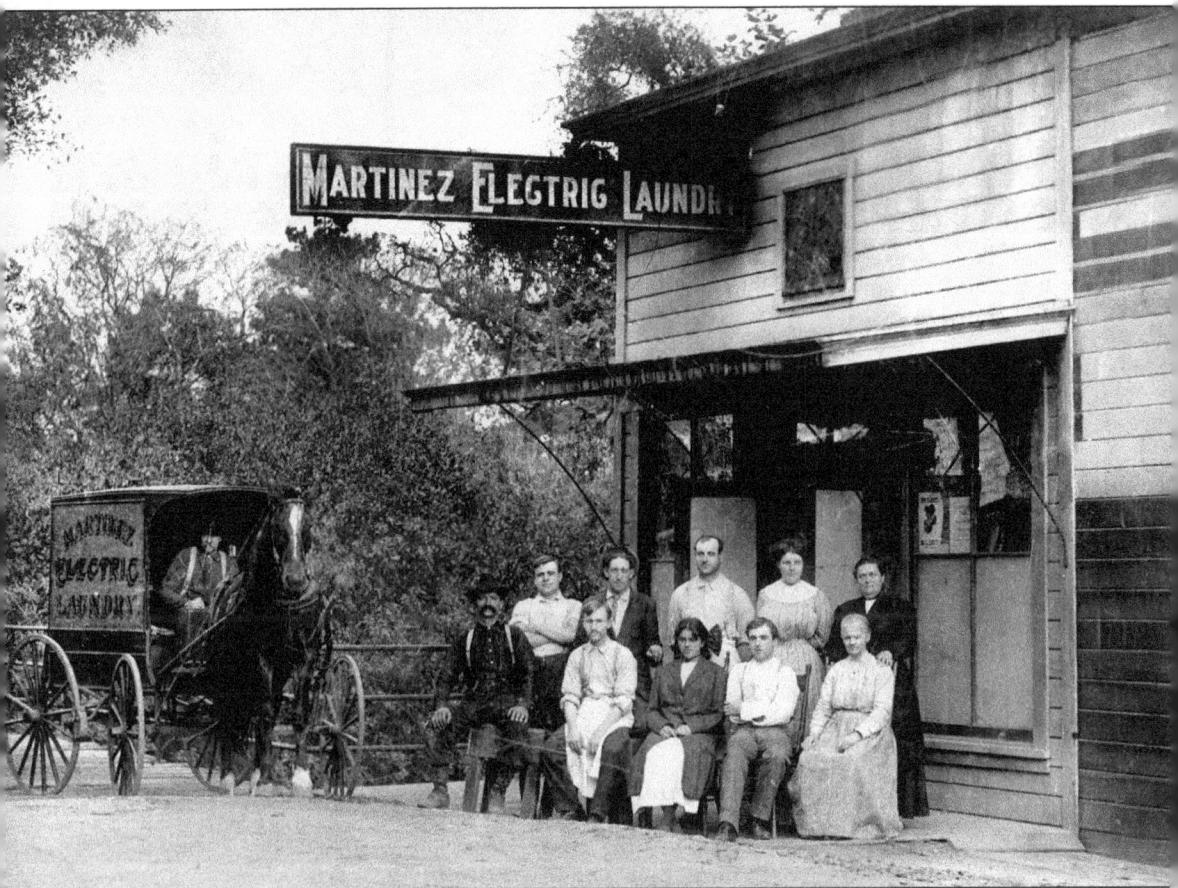

The Martinez Electric Laundry, pictured above with employees in 1900, was located at the corner of Estudillo and Ward Streets and made local deliveries. Purchased by Clement and Eugenie Arnaud, it was the forerunner of the long-lasting Elite Linen Supply Company with facilities for dry-cleaning and laundry.

The Martinez Furniture Company advertised in innovative ways in the 1920s. The owners put a loudspeaker on their delivery truck, broadcasting advertisements as it drove around town. It put up a billboard on Pacheco Boulevard around 1930. Note the orchards in the background.

The sign on the building on a flooded road announces a General Blacksmith and Horseshoer. This was J. Maloche's establishment around 1910. The hand-lettered sign reads "No Shoot'n," with the proprietor's name.

The Shelby family operated the largest of the Martinez stables in the early 1900s. This picture of their barn was taken in 1918.

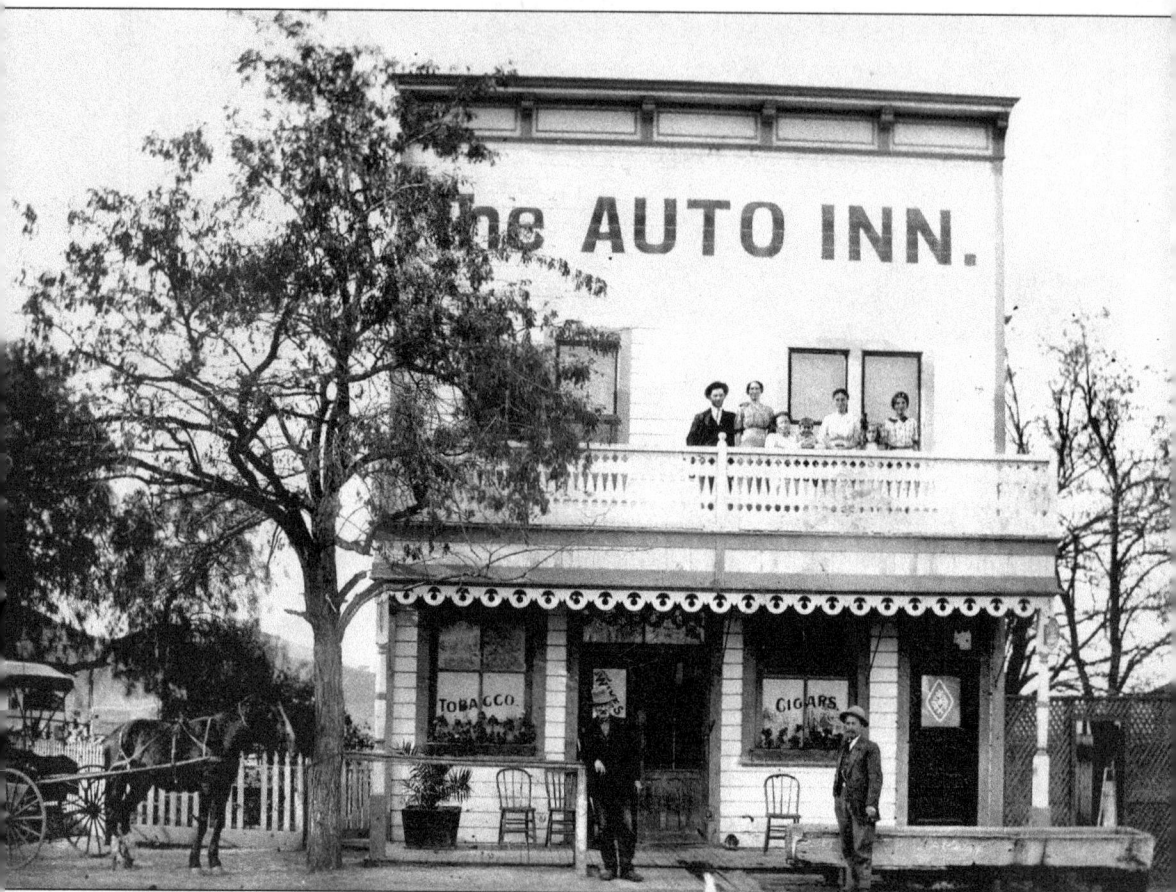

This photograph suggests a transition from horse to automobile. "Auto Inn" on Pacheco Boulevard provided its customers with a hitching post and a horse trough.

When horses gave way to automobiles, car dealerships replaced stables at the edges of downtown. DeRose Chevrolet is pictured here around 1925, with Charles DeRose, manager, and owner Jack DeRose.

Service stations and garages replaced the blacksmith shops. Pictured here is Allen's Garage, also taken around 1925. The building has been enlarged and now houses an automobile service and a golf cart sales and repair business.

The J.B.M. Building on Main Street, next door to McNamera's Tavern, pictured here in 1916, has served a number of businesses over the years. It currently houses a restaurant.

Beginning in 1902, Alhambra Natural Mineral Water Company, another of L.M. Lasell's enterprises, bottled water from a local spring in Alhambra Valley for distribution by wagon and rail to Northern California. A spur line from the Central Pacific tracks is pictured here in front of the plant, while a water wagon stands in the road. In the background is a water tank for steam locomotives.

Bull's Head Oil Company built the first oil refinery in Martinez in 1904 on the eastern edge of town, next to Mountain Copper (upper left). Martinez attracted this kind of enterprise because of its harbor and rail connections.

Associated Oil Company (Avon) began operations near Martinez in 1913, but the greatest change for the town resulted from the work of the Royal Dutch Shell Oil Company, which began construction of a plant the following year. It laid pipelines from the Coalinga, California oil fields to Martinez.

The Mountain Copper Company, "Mococo," built a smelter on Bull's Head Point in 1905. This was the first large-scale industry in Martinez. Byproducts were used in the production of fertilizer. By 1910 it employed nearly 300 men.

Byproducts manufactured at Mountain Copper were used in the production of fertilizers.

The plant operated night and day, every day of the year. The company continued to grow, employing nearly 300 men by 1910 and up to 400 men during the 1920s with a payroll of $500,000.

In this view of the construction of the Shell refinery, a steam shovel places excavated dirt on horse-drawn wagons to be hauled away. Trucks with the capacity to move such heavy loads were not yet in general use.

Shell workmen used horse-drawn equipment to level the land for building. Large numbers of animals were required to provide the horsepower that only a small number of bulldozers, scrapes, graders, and trucks would provide in later decades.

LANCASTER STUDIO
MARTINEZ

In 1916, the Shell Oil Company's refinery in Martinez was the largest in the United States. In this aerial view of the plant, Howard (Marina Vista) Street is located in the center left from the bottom.

This is an aerial view of Shell Wharf, also known as the marine terminal. It consists of a 40-foot-wide concrete wharf, 1,950 feet long, connected to the shore by a 1,900-foot-long wooden trestle. The two berths on the outer side of the wharf can accommodate tankers with a draft of 38 feet. The two inner berths have silted in and are unusable.

Pictured here is an oil tanker moored at Shell Wharf. Tankers both deliver crude oil to the refinery and take away refined petroleum products.

*Four*

# THE HOMES
# OF MARTINEZ

Louis Cass Wittenmyer was a businessman, landholder, county clerk, and the first mayor of Martinez after incorporation of the city in 1876. He built this redwood Queen Anne–style house with Eastlake detailing on Richardson Street in the 1880s. Many community leaders in the late 19th century chose house lots near downtown. Martinez builders of both grand and modest homes used local materials for the most part and followed styles in general use at the time.

The earliest residents in Martinez built homes in the Spanish Colonial tradition, which spread through the Southwest and California during the period when Spain expanded its settlements and continued under the governance of independent Mexico after 1821. The first ferry landing in Martinez was on the Martinez family land west of Alhambra Creek. Ignacio Martinez's second son, Vicente, built an adobe home in 1849 near the creek, perhaps on the site of a cabin he used during cattle drives. The home eventually became the property of John Strentzel. It stands behind the main house at the John Muir National Historic Site on Alhambra Avenue.

Jose de los Santos Berryessa married Ignacio Martinez's daughter Francisca and built this adobe home on the road to the ferry landing in 1849. Although it was primarily a residence, the building accommodated community uses for the next few years: city and county officers used part of it until the courthouse was completed, the Masonic Lodge met there, and Martinez's first teachers held school there. It was torn down after the earthquake of 1906.

A Presbyterian preacher by the name of John Cameron (sometimes spelled Camron) was among the newcomers to California from the eastern United States at the beginning of the Gold Rush in 1849. Cameron purchased two lots at the corner of Las Juntas and Green Streets and built a two-story brick home. This was the first brick building in the new town. The Camerons lived in it only briefly before moving on to Petaluma and Sebastopol.

Lafayette I. Fish, an innovator in mechanized harvesting equipment, was a wheat farmer in Diablo Valley and one of the founding members of the Alhambra Grange that built Grangers' Wharf, as well as one of the founders of the Bank of Martinez. He built this Italianate mansion, similar to town houses in Eastern and Midwestern cities in the mid-19th century, on the hill above the eastern end of Escobar Street in the 1860s. The redwood used in homes like this came from the Moraga area of the Oakland hills.

Beginning in the 1870s, successful landowners, businessmen, and bankers hired architects and builders who used ornate styles with complex rooflines, prominent window enclosures, and intricate decoration. John Tucker was a sea captain from Nantucket Island who arrived in Martinez in 1851, prospered from wheat farming, and built this home on the hill that became known as Island Hill, west of the town's center, in 1877. Ownership of the home changed several times. In the 1920s Franklin Glass, a postmaster, moved it down to Escobar Street where it still stands.

Michael Winslow, a farmer in Reliez Valley southeast of Martinez, built this small, simple, wood-frame home at about the same time as the Tucker mansion. It remains standing today. These homes were often on lots large enough for gardens and some livestock.

C.Y. and Byron Brown were sons of Martinez surveyor and judge Thomas A. Brown. They and their families shared this mansion on Ward Street until a dispute led them to split the place in two. Later the two separated houses were further divided into apartments until finally torn down in the 1930s when Safeway Stores acquired the land.

By the turn of the 20th century there were a number of large, decorative homes in Martinez, giving the town a prosperous, middle-class look with landscaped lawns and gardens and even a few carriage houses. Henry J. Curry built one of the most striking examples of Queen Anne Victorian architecture. He owned livery stables on Ferry Street and opened a funeral home as a branch of his business of hiring out horses and carriages. In the early 1900s he also served as county coroner. The home pictured here, built on the courthouse block in 1904, was razed for the construction of a county administration building.

Fishermen in the predominantly Italian neighborhood that developed near Grangers' Wharf and Alhambra Creek built far simpler homes. Pictured here is the DiMaggio home, where the famed baseball players Joe and Dominick were born. The family lived here for only a few years, however, before moving to San Francisco. This house no longer exists.

ALHAMBRA VALLEY 666

In 1881 John Strentzel began construction of a second home a little closer to town than his first in Alhambra Valley. He intended for his daughter and son-in-law to live in the residence with his widow, Louisiana, after his death. She continued to be active in Martinez community affairs until her death in 1898. Subsequently most of the property, shown here with vineyards and orchards, was sold, and the house changed ownership several times before being designated as the John Muir National Historic Site in 1964.

The Royal Dutch Oil Company used similar house plans in many parts of the world, including the tropics. In Martinez, the company housing was located on slopes above Escobar Street, on land that is now within the boundaries of the refinery, and in the area east of Pacheco Boulevard. A number of these homes still stand on the hillsides along Pacheco Boulevard.

The lots were large enough for vegetable gardens behind the cottages.

On Alhambra Avenue at G Street was a tavern and inn called the Alhambra House. John and Thomas McNamara built it in 1891 as a stopover place for travelers en route between various locations in the county—Alhambra was a main thoroughfare. John McNamara was a shopkeeper, builder of homes and apartments, investor in the Martinez-Benicia Ferry Company, founder of the State Theater, and mayor of Martinez for several terms.

Among the first buildings on or near Ferry and Main Streets were hotels and boarding houses serving both visitors and employees in the town's businesses and industries. The first hotel was constructed in 1850 by Josiah Sturgis and called the Alhambra Hotel. Pictured here is the Martinez Hotel, first built in 1887, its cupola providing a view of the harbor. The building was remodeled extensively in 1916 and destroyed by fire in 1939.

Hotel Oehm was built in 1915 (the photo dates from 1919). It became, successively, the Hotel Scott, the Travelers Hotel, and finally the River House apartments of today.

The Martinez Land Tract was the first subdivision in Martinez. William Thomas laid it out in 1914 on land west of downtown that he had previously used for the Bay View Pavilion, a park with a dance hall and baseball diamonds that had for years attracted visitors from all over the Bay Area.

This housing development was begun in the 1950s on land that was once covered with orchards. The view in the photograph is toward the south in Alhambra Valley, with Mt. Wanda to the right.

# Five

# THE LOCAL COMMUNITY

Main Street, shown here before it was paved, was first called Ruden, for one of the investors in town lots in 1850. The enterprises that lined the street made it a Main Street, and the intersecting Ferry Street (center of photo) led from and to the ferry, the town's first reason for existence. The intersection of the two streets may be the oldest continuously important town center in Northern California. The community of Martinez developed around it, generated and fostered by public services, churches, schools, sports, entertainments, and many voluntary associations. The population grew from 1,000 at the turn of the 20th century to 9,000 in the 1920s and 1930s.

Boards of trustees for the city of Martinez first met in the Berryessa adobe, then in business offices, and eventually in the county courthouse. Although Martinez was a county seat since 1851, and although the state gave Martinez a charter of incorporation in 1876, it was not until 1911 that citizens passed a bond issue for the building of a city hall. The city hall on Main Street, completed in 1912, provided space for city functions and for the town marshal, the constable, and the fire department.

The cornerstone of city hall contained a time capsule. When the wrecker's jaws lifted it out in 1956 during demolition of the building (to be replaced by a parking lot), city officials opened the capsule with some who had been present at the dedication of the building, including former sixth-graders who had written essays for the capsule. In addition to the essays, the contents included the *Daily Gazette*'s page one story about the laying of the cornerstone, a souvenir program, cards of local businessmen, and records of the vote for the bond issue that financed the construction. The contents are now on display in the Martinez Museum.

74

Citizens organized a volunteer fire department, Engine Company No. 1, in 1858 and reorganized it as the Martinez Hook and Ladder Company in 1871. Its services were essential—every few years a building or even whole blocks of buildings burned. The volunteers held fund-raisers to purchase needed equipment, such as the chemical machine shown here. Chemicals had to be used to control fires in the absence of public hydrants and cisterns. The Martinez Fire Department was eventually included in the county consolidated fire department. This view is of the back of the city hall, where the department was located.

James Rankin, a Scotsman who came to Contra Costa County as a coal miner, became a storekeeper and landowner in Martinez. He planted olive trees on part of his property, and some of these still stand in Rankin Park on the slopes west of downtown. He was elected sheriff in 1884 and served on the board of directors and later as president of the Bank of Martinez from 1893 until his death in 1902.

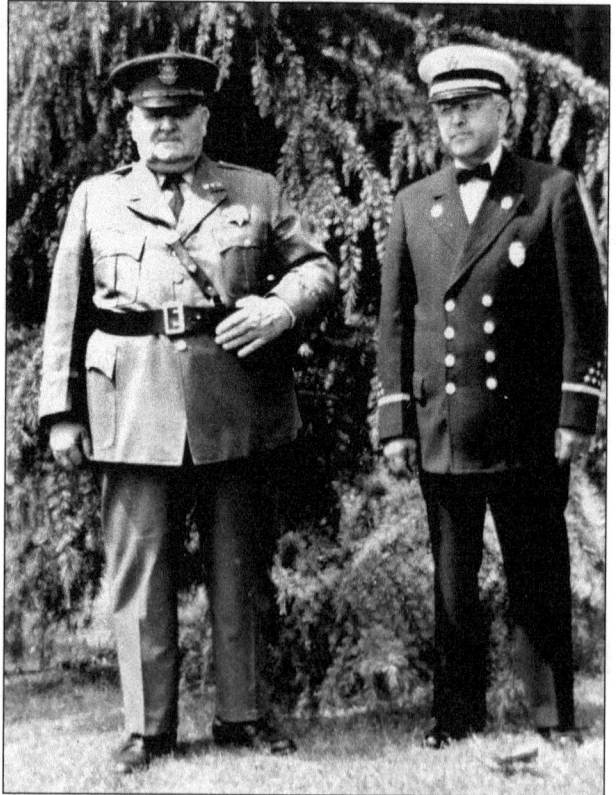

With a re-incorporation charter as a "sixth-class" city (based on population) in 1884, the board of trustees hired a town marshal in addition to the elected constable and separate from the county sheriff's office. The board also hired a night watchman for the business district. In the elections of 1918, Charlie Palmer was defeated for the office of constable, so the board created the office of chief of police for him. He went on to develop the Martinez Police Department, continuing as chief until his retirement in 1939. Pictured here is Chief Charlie Palmer (left) with Chief Toddy Briones of the fire department.

COUNTY HOSPITAL MARTINEZ CAL.

Following a state requirement that counties provide medical care for the poor, the county board of supervisors purchased land for a medical facility in 1880. Construction of a one-story wooden hospital began the following year. In the early 1900s wings were added and the hospital became a full-service institution. The private patients of general practitioners were admitted as paying patients until 1929, when the Martinez Community Hospital was built.

The "Little White House" has had a varied history that includes several moves and owners. Built as an adjunct to the County Hospital in the 1880s, it was later used by the city for a jail. It was then sold to the Bergamini family, who resided there for nearly 50 years. The First Congregational Church bought it in 1953 for use as offices and meeting rooms before Habitat for Humanity finally acquired it in 2004.

The oldest churches in Martinez are St. Catherine's Roman Catholic Church, Grace Church of the Methodist Episcopal denomination, and the Congregational Church. The first St. Catherine's Church, pictured here, was built in 1868; however, this photograph dates from the turn of the 20th century. Before it was built, Martinez Catholics belonged to the Benicia parish. An independent St. Catherine's parish was established in Martinez in 1874. The present St. Catherine's Church dates from 1940.

Martinez Episcopalians were also part of a Benicia church at first; Grace Church, shown here, was built in 1870.

Members of the Congregational Church, organized in 1874, met first in the Methodist Episcopal Church. They dedicated the church pictured here in 1885. After a fire, a new church was built on Court and Susana Streets and dedicated in 1927.

The first documented grave sites date from the mid-1850s, when Beverly Holliday and John Livingston, early landholders, bought and set aside five acres west of town for a cemetery. This land later became the Alhambra Cemetery. In 1862 Martinez women raised money to fence it. The founders of the city of Martinez, founders of nearby cities, people who were instrumental in establishing the county government, and several who participated in the formation of the state are buried here.

Across Carquinez Scenic Drive is St. Catherine's Cemetery, dating from the mid-1870s. It is the site of the graves of the Martinez family as well as of other pioneers. In recent years volunteers, including those who work with the Martinez Cemetery Commission (established in 1979), have maintained these cemeteries.

W.A. Rugg, pictured here behind his surrey with the fringe on top, established the first successful daily paper in Contra Costa County, *The Daily Press*, in 1900. It became *The Daily Gazette* in 1904.

The first newspaper in Contra Costa County was the *Contra Costa Gazette*, which began publication with this issue in 1858. The principal publisher after 1860, with various partners, was Roland R. Bunker, who came from Nantucket Island and built a home that still stands today in the neighborhood called Island Hill. The source of this photographed copy of page one, in the files of the Martinez Historical Society, is unknown; the first volume of the *Gazette* can no longer be found in any repository in California.

Newspaper carriers and office staff of the *Contra Costa Gazette* posed for this picture in front of the *Gazette* building.

In the office of the *Martinez Daily Standard* in 1912 is William R. Sharkey, manager, with the foreman, the pressman, and an apprentice. Sharkey served in the state assembly (1915–1917) and state senate (1917–1937) where he introduced bills for conservation. The Native Sons and Daughters of the Golden West named the square in front of the courthouse Sharkey Square in 1954 in tribute to William Sharkey's years of public service.

The first restaurants in Martinez were located in the hotels. One of the first in the Bay Area to use a residence was Paul's restaurant. Paul Pagnini bought James Kelly's two-story Italianate mansion on Alhambra Avenue in 1927 and converted it into a restaurant that acquired a reputation for fine dining. It continued to serve customers until 1981, when the building was destroyed in a fire.

Geneva ("Mollie") Spriggs and her husband, Sylvester, originally from Texas, opened a restaurant at the corner of Pacheco Boulevard and Blum Road in 1930. They offered a full menu, but the restaurant became best known for Mrs. Spriggs's chicken dinners made with poultry raised on the property. The restaurant closed in 1960 when plans to construct Highway 680 threatened it with demolition.

The Royal Theater in this street scene was the first of a number of theaters in downtown Martinez that attracted local residents and visitors in the 1910s and 1920s. It was located upstairs in Henry J. Curry's building (the McMahon-Telfer Building), which also housed retail stores and offices. Other popular theaters were the J.B. Maloche's People's Theater, the Novelty Theater, which offered musical comedies and silent motion pictures, and the Avalon Movie House, which opened in summer 1931.

"Papinta the flame dancer" (Caroline Hipple Holpin) was a popular performing artist in Martinez and in other cities of the United States and Europe around the turn of the 20th century. She used mirrors to reflect light from calcium arc lamps while she kept 100 yards of chiffon and silk in motion, giving the illusion of dancing with fire. She is buried in Alhambra Cemetery.

First opened in 1926, and remodeled in 1932 after a fire, the State Theater became an entertainment center for Contra Costa County. It scheduled vaudeville shows, motion pictures (silent at first and then with sound), and programs with such stars as Shirley Temple and W.C. Fields from the national circuit. Audiences came from the entire Bay Area in the 1930s. The Art Deco interior included floor-to-ceiling mirrors and 15-foot-high murals of Diana and Adonis. Although the building has been preserved, the murals have unfortunately been lost. It is currently used for public defenders' offices.

In the 1930s the "Early Days Fiesta" was an annual community celebration. It was put on by the Alhambra Alumni Club to raise money for school and town causes. Drill teams from all over Northern California participated, and dances were held at various places around town, including the Bass Club and the Curry (McMahon-Telfer) building.

Walter Bartlett directed the Martinez Choral Society (later the Martinez Music Club) in productions of operettas and other programs beginning in 1886. At first he rehearsed the performers, all amateurs, in Grangers Hall near the railroad station, using Louisiana Strentzel's piano.

The first Martinez opera company performed Gilbert and Sullivan's *The Mikado* at the Bay View Pavilion a number of times. This photograph comes from the production in 1912.

This roller-skating event was another locally produced entertainment.

Schools in Martinez regularly mounted their own productions. Alhambra Union High School put on *Lion and Mouse* in 1917. Productions by the senior class became a tradition. They were put on in the high school auditorium or, after the junior high school was built in the mid-1930s, in its larger auditorium.

Year after year adults and children gathered in downtown Martinez from December 1 to 24 to meet Santa Claus and celebrate Christmas. E.P. Vanni, who fashioned the "Fairyland" in Rankin Park, was often the Santa, and the Santa's house shown here is reminiscent of his structures. The tradition continues to the present, when Santa's arrival in town is welcomed with the Children's Christmas Light Parade.

In 1883 five young women organized a club to discuss literature and raise money for a free reading room, or public library. John Strentzel gave them a room in a commercial building he owned on Main Street, shown above. They raised money for books and established a library association with the support of Strentzel's wife and daughter Louie. The Strentzels donated a corner lot at Estudillo and Main Streets for a library building, and the library opened in 1896.

By the 1930s the library had more than outgrown its allotted space. A bond issue passed in 1938 made possible a new library building, which was completed in 1939.

Beverly Holliday, who had previously taught school in Illinois, began teaching in Martinez in 1850. Evidently he held school for only a short time, then opened a shop, and later turned to farming. The state legislature had yet to make provisions for taxation for local schools and thus to establish them as "public schools." As in many frontier communities, schooling was often informal, with parents paying a rate, or fee, per child and using their homes for schoolrooms. In 1862 John Swett, who later became part of the Martinez community, was elected state superintendent of public instruction and began a successful campaign to fund public schools. In Martinez a Ladies' Educational Aid Society raised money for school furniture for a room in the Masonic Hall in the 1860s and promoted the construction of a grammar school, finished in 1873. The Martinez Elementary School shown here opened in 1916.

Until the end of the 19th century Martinez residents who wanted formal education beyond grammar school had to travel to Oakland or San Francisco, where local taxes supported high schools, or cross the strait to Benicia, where Miss Atkins's Seminary (later Mills College in Oakland) offered instruction for young women. Efforts to start a high school in Contra Costa County communities were blocked by a state supreme court ruling that tax money legislated for grammar schools could not be used to support high schools. The state legislature provided for high schools in 1901, and a Martinez High School Association that was already in existence immediately introduced a ballot measure to create a high school district. John Swett was one of its organizers, and Julia Fish donated land at Henrietta and Court Streets for the first high school, a two-story frame building.

93

Pictured here are the first students and teachers at the new high school. There were three graduates in the class of 1904.

In July 1919 voters passed a bond issue for $175,000 to construct a new high school building. On March 24, 1921, a groundbreaking ceremony was held for the new Romanesque-style building that would be constructed on Smith Street (later Alhambra Avenue) at D Street at a cost of $185,000. Walls of the red-tile roofed, two-story, 250-foot-long structure were made of reinforced concrete. Built by Munson Bros. of San Francisco, it had an auditorium/gym that seated 850 people.

The park-like lawn of the high school campus invited relaxation. This photograph was taken in the mid-1960s. The building was demolished in 1971.

From its beginning, Alhambra High School promoted athletics. John Swett had been advocating gymnastics in the schools as early as the 1850s, when he was a teacher in San Francisco, and sports programs caught on in California's new schools as they were established. This photograph shows the Alhambra Union High School baseball team in 1910.

Townspeople promoted teams, too. Note the Martinez ties in this photograph dated 1914.

The Martinez Athletic Club seems to have played in individually chosen uniforms. Note the variety of shoulder pads. This photograph dates from the 1910s.

Some local businesses sponsored their own teams. This is the Lasell's women's basketball team in the early 1930s.

Italians brought the game of bocce to Martinez, playing at first in backyards. This photograph was taken in 1929 at the court on John Delchini's property above Alhambra Way near Brookside Drive. The court is bounded by railroad ties left over from the building of the Santa Fe trestle.

The City of Martinez eventually allowed play on the old Grangers' Wharf site. The first local tournament was held there in 1974, and a Martinez Bocce Federation was formed in 1976. Bocce became increasingly popular, and the federation was able to arrange for courts in the Martinez's Waterfront Park. This photograph shows the new courts.

The Veterans of Foreign Wars had a women's softball team in the 1940s.

The Martinez Women's Club raised money for local projects with performances such as this one of *Dancing Maids*.

The Masonic Lodge, organized in 1852 and chartered in 1854, is the oldest of the fraternal organizations in Martinez. It built this redwood building in 1859. This photograph shows the Lodge Building in its park-like setting on land the City later purchased for Susana Park. The Masons moved to a much larger building on the corner of Thompson (now Masonic) and Estudillo Streets.

Among the benevolent societies in Martinez was the Independent Order of Red Men, Cherokee Tribe No. 295, organized in the 1890s. In this photograph members are marching in a Decoration (Memorial) Day parade in 1916.

The Martinez Bass Club remodeled the old ferry, *City of Martinez*, for a clubhouse.

The Knights of Pythias was one of a number of benefit and insurance associations that spread across the United States with local lodges and chapters in the 19th century. They combined individual resources and promoted ideals of mutual assistance. Based on the ancient story of Damon and Pythias, the Knights emphasized friendship. The Golden Key Lodge No. 26 started in Martinez in the 1870s and met in its own building until a fire in 1904 forced it to move. This photograph of a costumed event was taken in 1910.

Businessmen, attorneys, educators, and other community leaders organized the Martinez chapter of the National Exchange Club, an all-volunteer service organization, in 1923. Charter members were from several Northern California cities as well as Martinez. Ralph H. Wight (second row, second from left), a city attorney, was instrumental in organizing the Martinez chapter. The club sponsored youth groups, including Boy Scout Troop 2 (later Troop 182), Cub Pack 182, and Brownie Troop 1221; donated money to scholarship programs; and for many years held a bicycle rodeo in Martinez.

Susana Park is a small, quiet park near downtown. It was home to many different trees from around the state and the world, including California redwoods, western cedar, and Portuguese cork trees. The small tree in the foreground was planted by children from the nearby Patchin's School. The grove in the back was the site of the first Masonic Lodge.

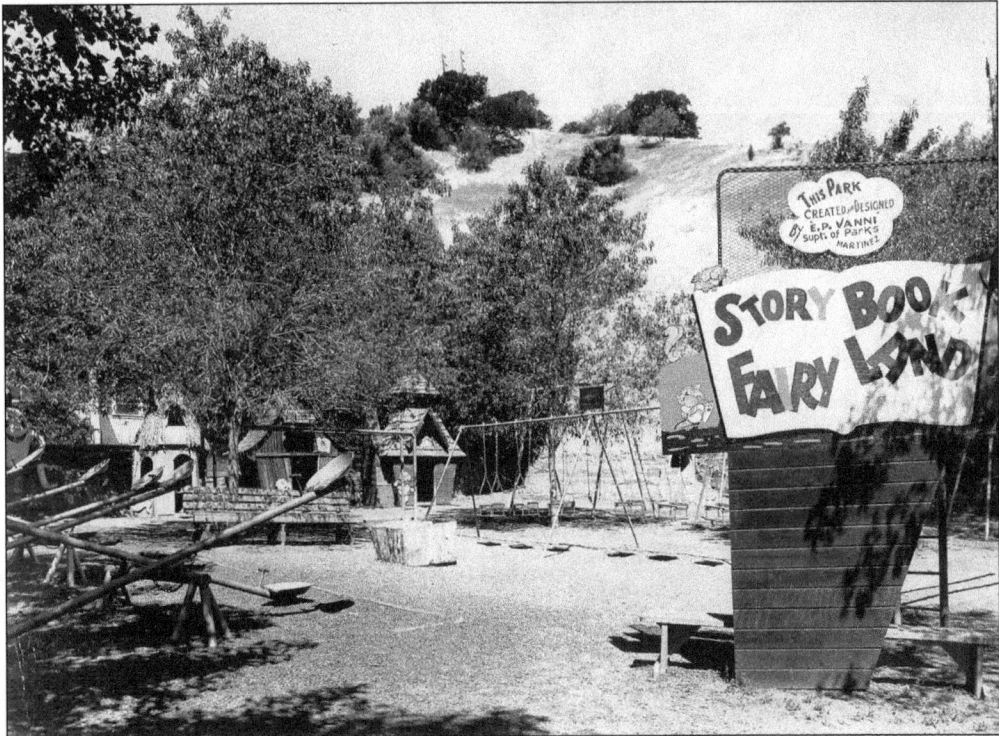

E.P. Vanni, superintendent of parks in Martinez, created Fairyland, a playground attraction at Rankin Park on the west side of town.

The local lodge of the fraternal society Woodman of the World had a drum corps that marched in parades and celebrations in the 1890s.

This photograph looks west along Main Street from Court Street in the early 1930s. The *Contra Costa Gazette* is on the right side of the street.

This is a similar view along Main Street in the early 1960s. Note that the utilities have been undergrounded, but parking meters and tall street lights now line the streets.

Ferry Street between Main and Escobar Streets has changed quite a bit in appearance since 1906.

In this photograph of the northeast corner of Court and Main Streets in the 1920s, the site of the original courthouse is near the center of the photograph.

In 1918 the city began paving Main Street. The streets were paved with asphalt, which first made its appearance as a paving material in the 1860s and gradually supplanted brick, stone, and wood blocks as the preferred paving material during the last half of the 19th century. After paving, citizens and merchants would no longer be subjected to streets of mud in winter and wind-whipped dust in summer.

Photographed here are the crew and the horses from Shelby's stables, working between Castro Street and Alhambra Avenue.

Flooding was a common problem because the business district was built on the flood plain of the Alhambra Creek, and the creek channel was narrowed to create more real estate at the top of the banks. Tidal action became an additional factor close to the waterfront. This photograph shows Main Street awash in the 1920s.

In the 1990s the downtown streets were still under water during the rainy season. Plans to solve the problem, of which there were many over the years, began to take definite shape in an Alhambra Creek Restoration Project, which was completed in 2002.

# Six

# Connections with the Wider World

Martinez celebrates the end of World War I with a jubilant parade. Never isolated, Martinez participated in national events and celebrations. And, as happened across the nation, advances in transportation—from waterways to railways and roadways to airways—changed the shape and life of the town.

A major highway project in 1965 created a new east-west highway south of the older, more established part of Martinez. This separated the original town from its newer developments. The housing tracts south of Highway 4 merged with those of Pleasant Hill and Lafayette. Pictured here is old Franklin Canyon Road on the left, while the new Highway 4 would now be to the right.

Various pieces of earth-moving equipment work on the construction of Highway 4.

In this photograph the John Muir National Historic Site is at the center, with Alhambra Avenue running past it from left to right. The train trestle runs along the left side of the new highway.

113

Martinez established a municipal airfield between the town and the strait in 1938 on tidelands that had been reclaimed over a long period of time. The airfield had a 1,800-foot runway, a hangar brought from the World's Fair on Treasure Island in 1940, and a flight school. Shut down during World War II, it reopened after the war as the Martinez Airpark. This aerial photograph was taken in 1950. The airfield closed in 1960, and Buchanan Field in Concord became the county's airport.

A deputy sheriff in the neighboring town of Crockett built the first hangar at Martinez Airport in 1933. The city dismantled the hangar in 1940, but the following year local air enthusiast Charles Beatie and Sam Calicura erected another one (pictured here), and Alameda Air Services opened a maintenance shop.

Frank Calicura stands beside the B-17G bomber he piloted with the 8th Air Force in Europe during World War II. The citizens of Martinez had raised $1 million in war bonds, so he was granted permission to name a plane.

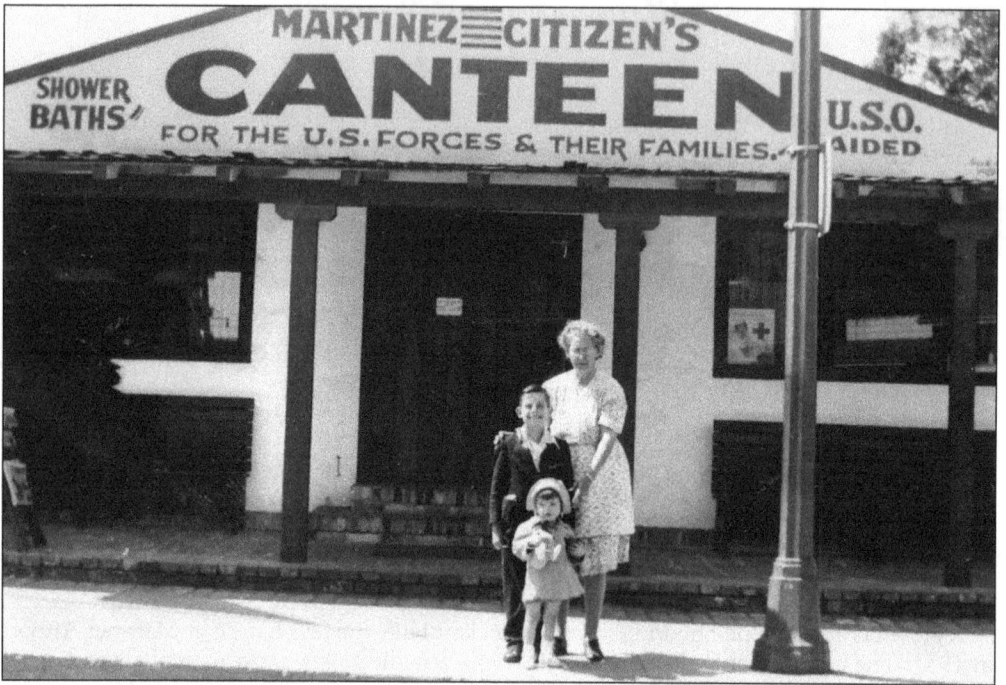

During World War II the USO—United Service Organization—operated canteens for servicemen and women. Entertainers donated their talents, women of the town prepared food, and the local canteen became a social gathering place. In Martinez, military personnel received everything free of charge, whereas many other USOs charged for what they offered. The building was located across Ferry Street from the railroad station.

The Kaiser Permanente Metals Corporation built Liberty Ships for the U.S. Navy at Shipyard Number Two in Richmond. The S.S. *John Swett*, named for the educator who laid the foundations of California's public school system (a Martinez resident 1895–1913), was launched on October 19, 1943.

A new train station replaced the old Martinez depot in 2001. One thousand local residents gathered for the dedication of the new station, along with prominent city and county officials.

This is the interior of the new station as it appeared in the summer of 2004. At this time the station was used mainly by passengers of CalTrans commuter trains as well as by long-haul Amtrak passengers.

# Seven

# MARTINEZ IN THE 21ST CENTURY

County government continues to be central to the life of Martinez. The complex of buildings shown in this photograph is only part of the presence of the county in the town. The 1903 domed courthouse with its high visibility from the surrounding area is gone; the courthouse is now the Finance Building (center), while the Hall of Records (right), built in 1933, has been used as a courthouse since 1965, and other offices are housed in the County Administration Building (back, left, and overleaf). Court sessions are held also at the A.F. Bray Superior Court, the new Family Court Building, and elsewhere in the county. The County also leases or owns additional office and storage space throughout downtown Martinez.

The County Administration Building is photographed here from the same perspective used by the photographer of the Curry mansion that replaced it (depicted in chapter four).

Mail carriers went by horse and wagon on their "appointed rounds" in the early 1900s.

A new U.S. Post Office building was constructed on Court Street in 1938. Maynard Dixon and his wife, Edith Hamlin, painted a mural depicting pioneers on the lobby wall the following year, with a commission from the federal program for art in public buildings. They had commissions also for murals in the California State Library in Sacramento and Coit Tower in San Francisco.

121

The scene in this photograph of Alhambra Creek is deceptively idyllic. Rains brought floods again and again to downtown Martinez. After an especially devastating flood over New Year's in 1997, citizens formed an Alhambra Creek Watershed Planning Group to evaluate options for control of frequent flooding.

This photograph shows restoration work on the creek bed and banks, looking south from Marina Vista toward Escobar Street. This project was designed to reduce flooding by a factor of five and to beautify the creek channel in the downtown area.

Martinez has more parks per capita and area than other towns in the East Bay. There is open space, as well as baseball diamonds, soccer fields, and hiking trails in the newer Hidden Lakes Park south of Highway 4.

This view of the Martinez waterfront in 2004 is in sharp contrast to 19th-century views. Note first the Martinez Marina, then the oil tankers at the Shell Wharf, and in the background, the railroad bridge and the Martinez-Benicia automobile bridge. Currently (2004), another bridge is being built east of and parallel to the railroad bridge to alleviate traffic congestion on the other automobile span.

Like Highway 4 to the south, Highway 21, which was widened into Highway 680, drew a line to the east of the older part of Martinez. Automobile traffic on both 4 and 680 bypass the town. This aerial view was taken from the Benicia side of the bridge, completed in 1962.

Voters in Contra Costa County authorized the formation of a junior (community) college district in 1948. One of the promoters was George Gordon, a Martinez attorney who became president of the first board of trustees. Two campuses were at first envisioned, one on the western, Richmond side of the county and the other more centrally located. The first classes were held in various locations, including Martinez City Hall and the courthouse. The central location for the east campus was the Martinez Elementary School (Boys and Girls Club). In 1950 the board purchased 100 acres south of Martinez for the campus that became Diablo Valley College. Administrative offices remained in Martinez, in the Borland House, until 1972, when the George Gordon Educational Center was built across Court Street.

In 1951 Superior Court justice A. Frank Bray Sr. of Martinez and collector Louis L. Stein planned the organization of a county historical society. Charter members included 134 Contra Costa citizens. As its first project, the society reprinted the 1879 book *Illustrations of Contra Costa County, California, with Historic Sketches*. Over time the society's collections of materials relating to county history grew and required larger quarters. The county board of supervisors provided a place in a vacated school in Pleasant Hill for a history center while the society looked for a permanent location. It found one in an old department store on Main Street in Martinez that had been Hilson's since 1913. With volunteers cataloguing and helping researchers with documentary, visual, and orally recorded information, along with continued publication projects, the Contra Costa County Historical Society and its History Center have become an important institution in Martinez. Part of the work and storage space is shown here.

When John S. Moore built a house on Escobar Street across from the courthouse in 1890, he planned that it would be a combination of dental office and residence. The style of the building was similar to that of others in Martinez and Bay Area cities at the time: a mix of Queen Anne and Carpenter Gothic elements of Victorian architecture, as shown in this photograph. Moore practiced his profession here for only a year, however, before his death, and the house became the home of his daughter and her husband, James Borland, and then of James's brother Robert and his family. Because of their long residence, the building has been known as the "Borland Home." In the 1940s a new owner converted the two stories into two apartments, and in 1949 the Contra Costa Community College District purchased the property for administrative offices. When the college district built a new administration building at the corner of Court and Escobar Streets, its officers planned to replace the Borland Home with a parking lot. Citizens campaigned to save the building from the fate of nearby Victorian mansions, which had given way to expansion of the offices of county government. In 1974 these citizens formed the Martinez Historical Society to take responsibility for the house and its restoration, with the goal of making it a museum and repository for the history of Martinez. The museum now houses an extensive collection of materials relating to individuals, families, and organizations that have shaped the history of Martinez, and welcomes researchers and other visitors to make use of these resources.

# FURTHER READING

Carroll, James G. *The Winemakers of Martinez USA*. N.P.: James G. Carroll, 1999.

Cohen, Andrew N. *Gateway to the Inland Coast: The Story of the Carquinez Strait*. Sacramento, CA: State of California, California State Lands Commission, 1996.

Collins, Katherine "Tina" Davi. *Pioneer Italian Fishermen of Martinez: "Nostri Pescatori."* Self-published, 1997.

Martinez Historical Society. *Martinez: A California Town*. Martinez, CA: RSI Publications, Inc., 1986.

Perry, Charlene McRae. *Martinez: A Handbook of Houses and History*. Pleasant Hill, CA: Diablo Press, 1998.

www.ingramcontent.com/pod-product-compliance
Lightning Source LLC
Chambersburg PA
CBHW050654110426

42813CB00007B/2007